This book is dedicated to:

Daniel Edward Bennett

Who impressed upon me
the weight of poems.

Introduction

In this collection of poetry, I, with a fearful respect for the inimitable masters of the past, have attempted to extract the universal from the individual experience, and humbly place these understandings into poems. You will find modern and archaic phrasing with the goal of capturing some of the magic of poetry. You will find rhyming and meter alongside more modern, freer forms. Human experiences of love, remorse, death, confusion, resilience, nature, and humor are explored.

I do not have the same educational qualifications that other writers of poetry possess, nor do I claim to be an authority on the subject. I have a very limited understanding on the mechanics of poetry, but I enjoy almost nothing more than reading it. Initially, much of poetry is difficult for me to understand, but after many re-readings, contemplating, and research, I find I can begin to appreciate the poem, as well as the poet. What I have placed in this collection are poems written in this spirit of appreciation, and at the exhaustion of my capacity.

It appears that modern poetry has become a sort of closed ecosystem in society. The inhabitants of this ecosystem produce, consume, discard, influence, and govern inside a bubble. I cannot accept that poetry is merely another hobby or subculture for enthusiasts, or a demographic for marketing. In my (admittedly naive) ideal, poetry is a cornerstone of culture where persons pursue it, not just for mild entertainment, but for the understanding and elevation of the self.

The exclusion of society from poetry, and poetry from society, is not malicious, but insidious. Poetry itself has not disintegrated, but interest in poetry has. Modern society is not stupid; our poetic faculties are just asleep. We must try to create art that is worthy of exploration by a society that has limited time and attention. Why would anyone spend their limited time on unfulfilling endeavors? (Don't answer that.)

We must try to write so that an isolated reader, who has come to a poem for their own private reasons, is not only able to feel the universal and timelessness, but is also given new paths for their mind to wander. We must not be pandering in our verse. We must try to produce resilient, resplendent poetry. For, when a curious reader tries a poem, and is haunted by the staggering emotions long afterward, they will no longer regard poetry in the same way.

If someone sits down to write a poem, they were moved to do so; and that is creation. The quality of the poem rests on the pureness with which it was written. Was the poem inspired by and written in accordance with the author's true self, or was it inspired by and written in accordance with a society-produced self? Or, worse yet, was the poem fashioned to please those that have formed and fostered a literary clique? Poems will be spectacular, timeless, and universal, when written for and by our true self, even if the topic is grim or peculiar.

We must be judicious and alert in our writing, but kind to ourselves when we have pushed our skills as far as possible to produce a poem. It will serve us all to remember that distinction in poetry rarely arrives before death, so we must write deliberately and honestly. Send for the stars, but converse with the moon while you wait. The moon is homely and humble, but also loyal, vigilant, and reflective of the sun's brilliance. We must learn to be humble, loyal, and vigilant if we wish to reflect reality's brilliance.

Lastly, I realize there is a stigma of pretentiousness associated with people that write and publish poetry. I assure you that I do not think that I should be considered a candidate for the pantheon of humanity's greatest poets, nor do I feel that these poems are superior to anything written today. I humbly presents these poems in hope that you will take the time to read, understand, and enjoy them.

- D.B.

Regard Me Not, O Muse

Contents

Foreword   1

Crystal Waters (A Ballad)   2

Bedtime Story   4

Dreams   6

Cemetery Maintenance   7

Walking By a Church in Early Spring   8

A Giraffe Dies   9

To Cameron   10

The Old Man and the Pond   12

A Worm in Love   14

First Autumn   15

The Universe   16

Jacqueline at White Rock Lake   18

This Madness   19

Lassitude   20

Taranis   21

Remorse   22

Observation   23

Black Hole   24

A Note   26

Benediction   27

In You   28

My Jacqueline   29

City Morning   30

Sunset in Key West   31

Suburban Pond   32

Journey   33

Cardinal in the City   35

Mexican Rose   36

Over the Hill   37

Remains   38

At a Cemetery in Winter   40

There's a Poem Around Me   41

True Love's Form   42

Regard Me Not, O Muse   43

Foreword

Though my abilities may be blunted
With cruelties loosed by my own discretion,
And I aim beyond the capacity
Of my narrow craft to shores of acclaim,
Allow me a few minutes of your life,
For that surely will be acclaim enough.
And if you consider what I have written,
You may also find that you have been
Compensated for your graciousness…

Crystal Waters (A Ballad)

Daniel leaves the pestering vacancies of wit;
His lassitude and slouch sloughed along the weeds.
He hefts what he has not learned to outrun or flit;
As a vagrant fingers the filth of wanton needs:

The bundle, rent from a swelling past of lessons,
Relics, trinkets, engorged with disapproving sighs;
Anxieties bestowed unaware, and questions
Left to die, yet still live! behind maturing eyes.

Curtailing his pace down the thorny road westward,
A gilded thurible chained to his leg is dragged;
Juddering and burping incense like a drunkard;
A ponderous pillar of smoke. A lead key swags

Prodigious from his neck, fitted for Splendor's door;
Whose hinge may never creak, though his bones surely shall;
For the flaring metronome ceases not the score
Time has composed for unwashed babes and burials.

His abandoned tree leans on a hill in the east,
Save a branch tangled in his hair, whispering low;
Maternal cants of muted dreams, and neuroses;
Tormenting the brain in a windy undertow.

Towards a mythic well, his clumsy feet strafe the path;
The mythic well, where crystal waters bathe the mind;
Preparing one for the Muse and the glorious wrath;
To ignite the banal tongue with glorious rhyme.

The chanters of heroic hymns came in their Spring;
In eras innocent of light-emitting spells;
But, since he held Pythia in his palm blathering,
He's left with a pilgrimage paved in walnut shells.

From out of the path into a clearing he plods.
The stately stone well stands majestic and alone.
Where he foresaw the teeming hosts of demigods,
He discovers a crushing multitude of none.

(Where are the champions that galvanized his heart?
Where are all the burgeoning minds electrified?
Is there no kindly sage with wisdom to impart?
No somber warnings for the insolence of pride?)

He approaches to draw his share of fabled dew.
The constellations peer through a cerulean veil.
His forefathers decompose to an earthy hue.
An exalted echo booms from the stony vale:

"You seek the crystal waters to loosen your tongue,
To descry colors only a few shall behold,
To dance in the distance where the comets are flung,
And to establish a myth ten-thousand years old.

"Alas, you *are* the mythic waters, haply moored,
To the salty warp and weft under easy sun;
While timbered mausoleums on the ocean floor,
Corrupt beside the remains of Leviathan."

Bedtime Story

Softly woven, the lamp light falls
In sentinel filaments; crushed
Beneath the sultry, mystic night
Breathing in the opened window.
Cicadian ascetics drone
Their wild-honey prophecy;
Visions of deprivation drip
From the windowsill where we play;
Pining for a bedtime story.
In joyous shrouds of youth, we are
Spared the barren anticipation
And the fungal anxiety
Of a Northern Winter (our ears
Perpetually wet in the Spring
Of our provincial life) and laugh
Into the Summer night seething
With Autumnal iniquities.

Our father, beloved of Demeter,
After felling the humble grass
Around the dooryard, gathers us
To my bed. He moves in honest
Exhaustion; leaving offerings
Of strength and spent acuity
At the feet of familial life.
He lowers himself between us.
The gravity of reasoning
Bows the mattress, and we tumble
Into his lap. With the somber
Charge of his paternal duty,
He reads from *The House that Jack Built.*
The sacred litany bounds
From page, to tired eye, to brain,
To voice, to rapacious ears. We
Bite our lips at the final
Benediction: our father red
Faced and squealing like a balloon
Deflating (while sweet sleep whispers

Seductively into his brain
Through the abysmal suspension
Of guiltless fatigue). I bury
My face in his shirt, breathing in
Gasoline and a mowed lawn.

Dreams

One has to be aware,
And keen,
Not to be seduced;
For one becomes confused
By listless wishes;
Vague apparitions;
Never to be subdued;
A hazy, rippling horizon;
Never gained,
Never rued;
As a mote
In the eye's fluid;
Always on the periphery.

Cemetery Maintenance

silent morning,
misted and lush.
quiet stones pierce the fog.

the weathered shed
yawns
combustion
and sour grass;

a thermos
conceals a name;

the trimmer
lopes
back
and forth.

one body
among thousands

lost
in a chilly desert
of grass
and stone.

Walking By a Church in Early Spring

The bricked and gilded glory
Of the neighborhood
Snorts and stamps
At my approach;
Wary of anyone without a tithe.

Through a snarl of naked trees,
A windsock whips to life;
Rippling in a Spring gust.
I whisper prayers to the pink and purple
Anemometer, as I pass;
It being the only pleasant sight
In the yellow and brown of a muddy March.

The consecrated men
On the rectory porch,
Swaying in the breeze,
Smile absolution
On my idolatrous head;
Their porch swing creaking like the pope.

The church looms above
Waves of shivering grass,
Weaving silence into the neighborhood.

A Giraffe Dies

Savanna wind smiles in passing above
The fanged predator and paranoid prey;
For all things were created in love;
Beautiful beings harmoniously placed.
The dry grass shivers for ice-cold death
Blows in like a storm graying the skies;
Down a sky-scraper neck, pulls a last breath,
Lays down dappled body and silently dies,
For the will of the world and accord of all
Who share the same air and burying soil;
For sorrowful kudus and their sobering call;
And sated lions with fresh, ruminant spoil.
Now returns the grinning wind to look upon
The speckled sustenance and the feeding lion.

To Cameron

Step forward young man and dispel
    Truths you were born to receive.
Expound the truth that's yours to tell
    Among crypts and withered leaves,
Of men and words you can't abide
Without an injury to pride;
Like one debating those that died
    That death is a reprieve.

Your youthful eyes survey the earth,
    All cratered and neglected;
For principles of phantom worth
    Our rotten hearts protected,
In the name of that and this,
As if we understood *the* kiss,
Was Judas in unblemished bliss,
    And had not defected.

Sometimes anger, sometimes greed,
    Is woven into reason;
And Wisdom sown as hapless seed,
    Is not reaped in a season.
But don't rely on other tongues
To teach you how your song is sung,
As well-respected men are hung
    For committing treason.

Your strength ignites a thousand flames
    That circle light around you,
But darkness goes by many names,
    That can and will surround you.
Draw your bow against the tide;
Lean in, for there is little pride,
In searching for a place to hide,
    When misery has found you.

Remember well, when you are lost
    In the tempest's angry bite,
And I am on my way to dust:
    I was moved to sit and write
For love of you and pride I've known:
These simple seeds of verse were sown,
So when in need, they would be grown,
    And they can be your light.

The Old Man and the Pond

I saw a man along the road,
On foot, struggling to drag a load;
Behind him bounced a blue canoe;
I would have stopped to help him too,

But I was tired, and work was tough;
And my temper had not enough
Of the price to fill my truck.
In vanity I wished him luck.

As I passed him, I looked to see
What kind of man he could be
Who has no friend to lend a hand
To haul his craft across the land.

Late sixties, maybe older;
Right arm missing at the shoulder;
His face was red, his brow was wet;
But on his mouth a grin was set.

I shook my head and laughed at him,
For that old man still wore a grin,
When in life he caught no break;
Nor friend to help, nor hand to shake.

That night, when all the stars returned,
Mirth ill-gained from the man I spurned,
Appeared in phantoms of remorse;
And so I left to dowse his course.

I knew a pond not far from here,
Where, I thought he should be near
By now, unless he keeled over;
Asleep forever in the clover.

I found him on that starry pond;
(The way a truth is found in song)
Laughing towards the Pleiades,
And spinning like a maple seed.

From the rushes I pondered why
A man should laugh into the sky,
When the sky refused to bless
His furrowed life with happiness.

But, he appeared the Chosen One,
And I, just a parable spun
To warn of petty arrogance;
Oh! how great the difference!

A Worm in Love

I once thought life a drudgery;
A blind evolution;
With the early worm eaten
In bitter confusion.

Ah! but now, if I was snatched
From the fertile loam,
I'd welcome it with joyous hearts
To soar above my home!

I'd wriggle in a furrowed cloud,
I'd sniff the tops of trees!
I'd taunt the fisherman below
That never hooked me!

And, if I'm lowered to a fate
Inside a fledgling mouth,
I will nourish slender wings,
And winter in the South!

First Autumn

The first Autumn with my lass,
    The apple boughs a-bending,
With blushing orbs of painted glass;
    Nary a fall portending.

The golden hues of early e'en;
    The silent leaves a-wending;
In ruddy skies a holy skein,
    For warmer climes is trending.

A mellow chill of wintry guile;
    Bitter Boreas southward bending;
His will rebuffed with her radiant smile;
    Her warmth his reign suspending.

We trace a fence with harvest crops,
    To a Shepherd's pasture lending,
His October grass cool and soft,
    For Summer's scorch a-mending.

Beneath a bower of an oaken copse,
    With roots downward sending;
Upon sewn leaves are fragrant notes
    For words in stone appending.

The Universe

In a distant age,
(Long before we donned the yoke of time;
Long before we raised a furrowed brow
And addressed the heavens;
Long before the briny bowers receded,
Obliging us
With incipient locomotion
To make haste from the waning waves)
Inside a forsaken corridor of despondent emptiness,
A remote star
Stretched its fiery tendrils;
Through fusion of elements unknown,
To grope the mute vacuum
For something more to illuminate than
Gaseous ennui and cratered bodies.

Six months ago
As we held each other;
(An immediate and assured attraction that vexes all physics)
With your body, your breathing, your peacefulness
Sending me into noiseless rapture;
The as yet unperceived photons of light
Were still bounding through an austere expanse,
Three trillion miles from your bed.

Today, as I sit across from you
Reading this poem aloud,
(My nerves ensnared in a quaking stillness,
Because your sanctifying presence reveals
A knowledge and wisdom much deeper than
My understanding will comprehend;
Because you are the Buddha's highest thought;
Because you are the Christ's upturned eyes in prayer;
Because you are the contentment in an awakened soul)
I look up and see glints and shimmers of joyous light
Swirl in your eyes.

Through numerical nuance and arbitrary precision;
Across a distance that tatters the imagination;
The lonesome star,
Whose existence was devoid of any purpose,
Save for the balance of an indifferent vastness;
Illuminates your eyes,
And in doing so,
Illuminates the entire universe.

Jacqueline at White Rock Lake

Jasmine clouds on a summer's day collect,
Above our bodies ambling 'round the lake,
Ceasing their drift to casually inspect;
Quite unaware of the scene they make.
Usurping their regard your beauty deigns;
Enacted without vanity's design;
Luring them until they dissolve in rains,
In their despair of being left behind.
Nimbus sorrow cascading in dark wind,
Exalts you beyond the praises of men.

This Madness

This madness that collides colossal spheres,
That ebbs and flows in the synapses,
Pushing the brush against the canvas,
Or a pistol between the teeth,
That inspires the renunciate to leave his family,
Or the martyr to hold a flame-licked,
Solemn face in stolid disobedience;
This universal madness,
Slings my horizonless existence
Into obedient orbit around you.

This madness that draws the timber up from the soil,
That scorches and revives the sibilant grasses,
Leading herds of ruminants in perpetual pursuit,
Or improvident nations to famine,
That ignites the vibrating canticle of insects,
Or creation to resist the dogged mania of malignant progress;
This pervading madness,
Settles my erratic revolutions
Into measured circles around you.

You,
Pulling at my oceans,
Endlessly rocking my axes;
While I admire at a distance;
Draw me irretrievably closer
To a delicious doom.

As you wind me tighter in my revolutions,
I fear no other collision;
Your discerning gravity sweeps away
Titanic satellites,
As you wait, composed and patient.

Lassitude

When Cassie's chair
Is observed
Balancing on the steeple,
And apologies for early nights
From forlorn bells
To faithless people
Blithely tumble through foggy streets,
My soul retreats
Between the covers of a book,
And indolence denies a look,
What heroic verse my soul betook,
To assume disgrace, and remain,
'Til the doleful bells grow still again.

Taranis

In a god-fearing land,
Septic innocence
Lulls the angry crash
Of atrocities
Upon a darkened,
Peaceful shore.

A stretched rope
Hangs hushed and still.

Tortured flames
Pine release from
Gnarled morality.

Whispered pleadings
And muted sobs
Collapse in the shadows.

Taranis has fallen silent.

Remorse

His darling wife pursued her dream;
Her dream took on a driving force,
That plied the water of her stream
To charting an unwonted course.
    While she presumed support from him,
    His leaves blushed on a tender limb.

He loved her. God, did he love her!
A gem in humanity's crown!
But he grew a cloud above her
And carelessly thundered it down;
    Impatient winds and lashing rains
    Surged her banks and submerged the plains.

She bore her dream, but her way was lost;
Like in a wood where leaves are stripped;
Scattered and swirling; tempest tossed.
The blissful dawn where sunlight tripped
    Upon the hills, brought to his sight
    That he was wrong and she was right.

The color faded from the land;
A sickening slate, when his wife,
Gathered his words in lovely hand,
Sharpened the hard words like a knife,
    To shred the tender words he'd laid
    At her feet as repentance paid.

Lo! Remorse is keen when what's done,
Is done; when love is in splinters;
When the heart is a fallen sun,
Buried 'neath unbroken winter;
    When the preaching of reap and sow
    Is mocking like an April snow.

Observation

From the altar of truth,
Casted in capitalist plaster;
Down the unnavigable
River of apostasy,
To the sordid orphanage
Of abandoned promises;
Where the lips of babes
Have ordained partisans;
And suckle at tradition's
Withered breast, go the
Teeming progeny of idealists.

Black Hole

...wild uproar
Stood ruled, stood vast infinitude confined
                                        - Milton

Long, long I stood observing the night sky.
The immaculate pattern of rural stars
(Undyed by the luminous filament
That betrays a city to highway cars)
Looked down upon me as Magi meant
To behold salvation; they only sighed.
Though far from the city, I could not slough
Its savage inflections that warped my heart,
Cracked my crystal gaze of serenity,
And left me,
With my blank face upturned to infinite
Questions. Oh, I was sorry I even tried
To see what a philosopher might see.
I found discontent (or perhaps it slept
Inside me; lulled by the frantic rumblings
Of a municipality; and woke
Like a bat in the attic when quiet crept
In through the chinks), but a philosopher
Would find glorious frustrations, and joke
That all these internal bumblings
Should not be disdained, for they proffer
A peek into a dwindling faith in God.
I could not speak for humanity's faith.
I could not even speak for *mine* that night;
The belted trinity no longer awed.
I gazed up in expectation only.
I stared a while longer, then bowed my head.
"Endless space above for endless questions
To fly and tumble about; shooting stars
Without a temporal flame for detection,
Or a tail to pinch for close inspection
While it wriggles in fright,"
I mumbled to myself as I returned
To my truck (dark and patient as Charon's

Bark), when a thought, lighter than a photon,
Settled on my mind. O, how my heart burned!
I now observed the infinite ink above,
And was not put under a morose spell,
For I knew that all this inky chaos,
Will return to the ink well!
Black hole indeed! A godly gift of love!
What can escape a love like that?
Not galaxies, nor shooting stars,
Nor tumbling endless questions,
Nor constellations, nor evil, nor light,
Nor thoughts lighter than light.

A Note

Darling,

        This is just a note to say
That at the end of heaven's day
(When the weary worshipers plod
To chambers never far from God),
The angels sweep the streets of gold,
Then light the lamps for inbound souls,
And with their obligations through,
They disappear to dream of you.

Benediction

When I wake to find the burgeoning opulence
Of Autumn rotting in the dismal mud;
When frigid branches scrape the arid winds;
When darkness grows bolder, circling nearer
The perfumed fortress of the heart;
When dreary mornings find me shivering
Against the bleak prospects of day;
When invisible steps of thought lead past doors
Forever fastened against me;
When fearful, swelling clouds of unread books
Choke the flame of study;
When morbid visions pitch across the ceiling
In the restless, vapid night,

I only need to look upon you sleeping, angel-like,
Wrapped warm in your wings;
Or find you radiant, effusing pleasure,
In your just-woke smile;
Or watch you at your desk, shimmering
In beautiful concentration;
And the yoke of wretchedness,
With its myriad titles: satan, ego, karma, depression, sin,
Lay vanquished before your unwitting benediction.

In You

All I attempt is left unfinished:
Dismal vaguenesses descending
Into half-written thoughts;
Phantom desires dissolving
Into an ever-widening wind.

But, you enclose all.

Beauty cascading from heaven;
Perfect soliloquies sprouting
In sovereign nature;
Gossamer visions sighing into mist;
All abide in you.

My Jacqueline

I crawled up a mountainside weary and torn,
    To hear what was told in the wind;
Far from the burden of labor and greed,
        It whispered Jacqueline, and Jacqueline again.

I tramped silent miles in a pathless forest,
    To interpret the sunlight among the trees;
Amidst the timbered cathedral dazzled
        Jacqueline's name in the glinting leaves.

I pursued a myth into sacred lands,
    To where the blessed honey drips;
In orchards 'neath a perfect Sun,
        Only to taste my Jacqueline's lips.

I stole away to where the wild roses bloom,
    To worship with both gods and men;
The darling flower; heaven scent,
        And lo, the fragrance was my Jacqueline's.

I stood outside in a summer's rain
    To discern the touch of nature's grace;
The living waters to the withered grass,
        Was Jacqueline's kiss upon my wearied face.

City Morning

On a city Spring morning, 'ere you rise,
When windshields and stop lights glisten with dew,
I begin the day with rebellious eyes,
While my mind has remained in bed with you.
The trash truck rings the dumpster's evening knell,
As early risers grudgingly plod their way.
I'm sure in my absence, all would be well,
If I retreat 'til tomorrow's today.
But, as Dawn's advanced guard breaches the sky,
Churlish resolve my uprising subdues;
I lay sweet thoughts on your pillow, and sigh,
Slip on my jacket and lace up my shoes.
    Lo! let the scant trees wilt, if I, in remiss,
    Ever leave you without a silent Spring kiss!

Sunset in Key West

O sweet rapturing sun descending!
Take dictation upon your slanting beams.
Drape my simple thoughts upon all you awaken
With your irresistible brilliance!
Say that we passed a pleasant, peaceful day here.
Tell everyone I send momentous love, and entertain no
    bitterness.
I bestow on you mortal cheerfulness; a gift to endure long
    journeys.

As you pour immense your limpid glints into blinking eyes,
Immerse the soul in your immortal reasoning.
Remind the worried and distraught
That the Earth receives babes and meteors
With the same deliberate calmness.
Do not fail difficult or entrenched persons;
Melt disparaging innuendos in your illustrious, fiery beams!
Bend odorous bigotry through a clear light;
Will its angry visage to refract into phantasms of color!

At dawn I will wait by warm, green waters,
To read encouragements and lessons drafted far hence;
Etched across your illustrious flame!

Suburban Pond

In low pasture reposed, a dripping god,
Circumscribed within a concrete noose;
The revivalist balked; his soul unsprung;
Thou silent cancer a descending sluice.

Dazzling, thou liquid chandelier, retards
Druid delusion—thy quivering breast
Pocked with ephemeral jewels extolling
Clean nature, and rebuking wilderness.

Oh aqueous platform thou animate
Seething desire until we descend,
Impetuous, upon thy scuttled bed,
To lave our souls in Lethe sleep again!

Journey

Beauty presides o'er this evening
As we languidly repose,
Observing the dissolution
Of photons in the western sky.
I note the remarkable way
You withdraw into yourself
When all is silence between us.
Serene, you drift beyond our porch,
Beyond the humming street light,
With its myriad insects
In frenzied prurient pursuit,
Beyond darkened trees obtrusive,
Into the spattered, starry sky.

The enfolding, secretive night
Delights and approaches softly
Your immaterial person,
Discharging sweetened atmosphere
To dissolve serrated edges
Tempered in the flames of worry.
The future, tenacious, fluid,
Perfumed with hope, flutters inside
The swirling daydreams of your mind.
And though the knowledge of phantom
Time, quick dissolving, bristles in
The background of beautiful dreams,
The all-reconciling darkness
Retrieves from distances immense,
Your childhood, left to float among
Snuffed stars and broken galaxies,
To remind you of innocent hopes,
Faithfully ministered by the
Incorruptible universe.

As you dream with the fickle crowd
The baleful vision of fortune,
You betray subtle diffidence
Toward the manic rapaciousness

Of material luxury;
Your measure of success lies not
In finite distances acquired,
But in redolent rhythms,
And sweet melodic progressions
Arranged against your tempo of
Undisturbed contentedness.

You return to me with a blink
And a smile. In your face I read
A truth whispered into your soul
By a generous universe
I have only beheld in you.

A Cardinal in the City

The tiresome veil of traffic
Smothers my morning sill,
But threading this noisy fabric,
Is a cardinal's dewy trill.

With wisdom in his whistle,
And heraldry in his plume,
He bestows to me a trestle,
To span the clamoring gloom.

His freedom leaves no cup to fill,
Hence no persons to beguile,
So he freely plays celestial
Lays, and I freely give a smile.

    Lo!
The vermillion-throated muster,
More delicate than the bird,
Supplants the odious bluster
Of combustion's manic herd!

Mexican Rose

We witnessed nature wax glorious charms
In heaps of flowers spilling o'er her arms.

She chose the fairest to sweeten our view,
But she renounced them all in seeing you.

"An immaculate bloom without tether
To the soil, the season, or the weather,"

She sighed, as you wended so fragrantly
Among her blossoming progeny.

A flower beyond all flowers conceived
By her, and lo! as all heaven perceived,

Beyond what grows in their downy bowers;
A Mexican Rose; queen of all flowers!

Over the Hill
(After Contemplating the Strength and Resilience of M.P. and J.J.)

Friends, *Over the Hill* is a paltry phrase
To measure the breadth of one's nights and days.
What youth opines in derision or mirth,
Hints at possessing a diminished worth,
But heed the wisdom attained in the climb,
And the vistas impressed upon the mind!

Are there no thoughts of what else is implied:
The journey's pleasant on the downward side?
Pause your mad ascent; your burgeoning skills,
To take sober view of the surrounding hills:
Observe the descent on a yonder face,
As the perils and hazards come on apace!

Gravity's draw, surely felt in ascent,
Pushes one headlong when at the descent.
A sturdy staff hewn from maturity gained,
Does little to counter calamity's strain;
And it can't cheer one whose spirit is low,
When the mind's transfixed on what lies below.

Now glares an allusion youth gaily portends:
Each hill that is traveled must come to an end;
For Respect, though a word youth merely hears,
Manifests as annihilation draws near.
Prepare dear fledglings, with aerie gaze and soaring pride;
To hail fierce Respect grinning on the other side!

Remains

Real are the dreams of gods
— Keats

Long have you reposed upon a lithic
Wave—above the dread, ephemeral pound
Of cresting, thunderous seas terrific—

Washed in refulgent blue and lightly downed;
Winnowed by ethereal winds and left
A marrowy splendor daubed dusky brown.

None can say if ever there was, bereft,
A primal mate that sighed a monody,
Or if a sacred quarry stone was cleft

To spurn the shadows of mortality,
For you are nearer to waking Muse,
Than you are to Socratic irony.

Thin element respires through ribs now fused
To crags dissolved in everlasting gape,
As distant stars converge in somber hues,

Remarking the pitiful sight you make;
Descending, fain to light your aerie vault,
And to imprint your constellation's shape.

Sprung from the mountain; a celestial cult!
Tended with votives of infinite flame!
Yet immortality lies on a fault:

By discerning the stars before your brain
Could fathom an ear for a fervent prayer,
And leaving no mark to recite your name,

Immortality's weight is yours to bear
Without the illusion of mortal thought.
Although abandoned in depleted air,

Inside your skull sweet mysteries unknot;
Diffusing in silent mandible sighs:
That a single simple sun has wrought,

A lilting commensurate paradise,
But a trillion distended stars have burned
Away the worship of the morning skies.

O antecedent, your children have spurned
Your nascent deities of savage birth,
And in our crowing madness we have turned

More barbaric gods loose on the earth!

At a Cemetery in Winter

The foregoing cannot describe it well
Enough to convince my heart to fear it,
Though silence is a conspicuous tell,
That haunts and forecloses on my spirit.

The stones refuse a kindly word beyond
The epitaphs inscribed upon their brow,
As if the frigid bones they're placed upon,
Could hear the whisper of the falling snow.

There's a Poem Around Me

There's a poem around me;
I can hardly tell for sure,
If it grew inside me,
Or slid below the door.

It's vague as a slight nod
From a stranger's head,
Or an answer sent by God
Without words being said.

I try to touch its essence,
But it eludes my mind,
As if an inky presence,
Is putting *me* in lines!

True Love's Form

Not in joyous day my pleasure resides,
    Where trees gambol and the cardinal calls;
    As a smile, the sun insensibly falls,
And a weary traveler must turn aside
In tepid lucency of night's false pride,
    And tease a memory from distant halls
For floating the dismal darkening tide.

Nor in fortune is my pleasure at play,
    Where whims and entertainments are granted;
    When Affluence dances, those enchanted,
Deliver their heads upon silver trays,
And dissipate to keep their thoughts away;
    For Greed is aware the level's slanted,
And sickened ennui dissolves the day.

Nor in poems can my pleasure repose,
    Where glories and passions perfume the page;
    For like the ocean, emotions may rage,
But drowsily ebb as the book is closed;
The poets and passions soon decompose;
    And the reader's memory fades with age,
Like the North Wind's influence on the rose.

Nor can my pleasure be retained in truth,
    That lofty tower in the minds of men;
    From an apex of reasoning, descend
To bequeath cliches to credulous youth,
Who inherit the structure without proof;
    Which chiseling Time leaves a hoodoo, then
With a whisper can be toppled, forsooth!

My pleasure exists in my true love's form,
    Whose radiance absolves the wretched night;
    Whose virtue weakens the rapacious sight;
Who provokes the Muse to perpetual storm,
Witnessing raptures of womanly charm!
    Who summons the verities to alight,
Amidst my pleasure in the true love's form!

Regard Me Not, O Muse

Regard me not, O Muse! Do not
Dawdle o'er awkward instruments
That squawk and clank pretentiously.
Do not animate idle scythes
In darkened corners of warped sheds
—Where spangled sunset permeates
The thin swirl of chaff from harvests
Improvident and ruefully
Remembered—no longer brilliant
Enough to clear away the weeds
With a persuasive hush, or call
Forth feathered words to settle upon
The gorgeous morning thoughts of her.
Instead, release your pious ache
Of silent lust, and desire
Protracted, into the fertile
Wind. Flood the sea air with madness;
Unrelenting, pure madness sparked
From the sound of her pleasured sigh.
Let churlish Sirens dash their heads
Upon igneous pride and leap
Aboard sure-fated ships to lay
Themselves, dower-less, at the feet
Of misty-eyed, feigning sailors.
Tell of her resolve. Tell how her
Childhood dreams, wet in the misted
Horizon, led her, nigh-pathless,
From the humble well of her home.
Sing of Odysseus, aided
By the gods, and what he vainly
Achieved, then recite her journey.
Sing her successes and the pride
Of her family; how she draws
Water still from the humble well.

Praise the blooming, not the flower,
For many are the well-beloved
Tales adorning the halls of time,

But those most enchanting are found
To be still unfolding. She may
Never rest upon a laurel,
Or rock upon an easy-chair,
And so be it! For potential
Is interminable in her!

Rend the mysteries of language
To pour a draught of true passion
Upon her fane! Tell of beauty
That possesses man, then compare
What thou perceive in her brown eyes!
Sing of her kindness. Sing how she
Cast her benevolent eye on
A simple suitor, and chose him
To keep watch over her temple.

Remind us of the oscillating
Stars as we grind out lonely days;
Raptured by our loathsome worries.
Remind us that they have observed
The vile deterioration
Of humanity's bountiful
Love. Whisper in each sleeping ear
That the sentinel stars have found
New hope in her. Uncouth, storming
Inside solemn churches, blaspheme
A lesser god; for to look upon
Her is to break from crumbling faith;
To lie in green pastures beside
The resurrected Christ. Announce
How my love for her shall persist
Long after all is silently
Still. When the last particle sighs
In death, and the fate of matter
Is left to God, *she* shall create
A new existence. Loose, O Muse,
Your passionate phrase everywhere!
Erupt ponderous flaming fumes,
Or arrive as gentle as breath
Upon a mirror, so one in skill
Superior can heed Your notes

And sing her praises in language
That expounds her peerless essence,
For I shall be humbly grateful,
And lay down my pen satisfied!

Thank you for taking the time to read this little book.

If you enjoyed these poems, please let me know.

contactdanielbennett@gmail.com

Made in the USA
Coppell, TX
23 February 2026